FIREFIGHTER HEROES

FIREFIGHTERS ON THE WATER

By Spencer Brinker

Consultant: Beth Gambro
Reading Specialist, Yorkville, Illinois

BEARPORT
PUBLISHING

Minneapolis, Minnesota

Teaching Tips

Before Reading
- Look at the cover of the book. Discuss the picture and the title.
- Ask readers to brainstorm a list of what they already know about firefighters. What can they expect to see in the book?
- Go on a picture walk, looking through the pictures to discuss vocabulary and make predictions about the text.

During Reading
- Read for purpose. Encourage readers to think about what firefighters on the water do as they are reading.
- Ask readers to look for the details of the book. What are they learning about what firefighters on the water need in order to put out fires?
- If readers encounter an unknown word, ask them to look at the sounds in the word. Then, ask them to look at the rest of the page. Are there any clues to help them understand?

After Reading
- Encourage readers to pick a buddy and reread the book together.
- Ask readers to name two things firefighters on the water do. Find the pages that tell about these things.
- Ask readers to write or draw something they learned about firefighters on the water.

Credits

Cover and title page, © curraheeshutter/iStock and © RichLegg/iStock; 3, © Steven Parks/Adobe Stock; 5, © surasak petchang/iStock; 6–7, © Sheila Fitzgerald/Shutterstock; 9, © Sergii Figurnyi/Shutterstock; 10, © Robert V Schwemmer/Shutterstock; 11, © Larry D Crain/Adobe Stock; 12–13, © Gertjan Hooijer/Shutterstock; 14–15, © ollo/iStock; 16–17, © kjerulff/iStock; 18–19, © kcapaldo/Adobe Stock; 21, © John M. Chase/iStock and © RichLegg/iStock; 22, © joshuaraineyphotography/iStock; 23TL, © Kathy images/Adobe Stock; 23TR, © OlgaMiltsova/iStock; 23BL, © Alberto Masnovo/iStock; 23BR, © HASPhotos/Adobe Stock.

See BearportPublishing.com for our statement on Generative AI Usage.

Library of Congress Cataloging-in-Publication Data is available at www.loc.gov or upon request from the publisher.

ISBN: 979-8-89232-719-0 (hardcover)
ISBN: 979-8-89232-769-5 (paperback)
ISBN: 979-8-89232-806-7 (ebook)

Copyright © 2025 Bearport Publishing Company. All rights reserved. No part of this publication may be reproduced in whole or in part, stored in any retrieval system, or transmitted in any form or by any means, electronic, mechanical, photocopying, recording, or otherwise, without written permission from the publisher.

For more information, write to Bearport Publishing, 5357 Penn Avenue South, Minneapolis, MN 55419.

Contents

Fire at the Dock 4

A Fireboat and Its Tools 22

Glossary 23

Index 24

Read More 24

Learn More Online 24

About the Author 24

Fire at the Dock

The boat is on fire!

Flames are on the dock, too.

Who can help?

We need firefighters!

Many firefighter heroes work on land.

Others work on the water.

Water firefighters speed to the dock in a **fireboat**.

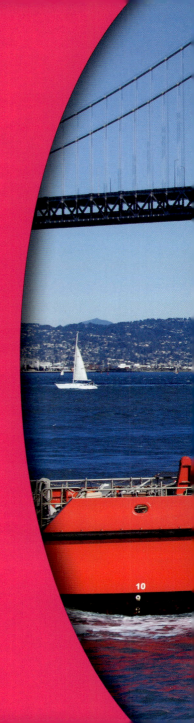

A fireboat

The fireboat is big.

It brings the heroes to the fire.

The boat also has the tools the firefighters need.

The fireboat **pumps** water from below.

The water goes up to the boat's **nozzles**.

These shoot the water far!

The heroes point them at the fire.

A nozzle

The heroes are putting out the fire.

Then, they see something.

Someone is trapped on the boat.

The person needs help!

The firefighters get close to the boat.

They take the person away from the fire.

Now, the person is safe.

Sometimes, there are fires at sea.

These heroes go to help.

They rush to boats that are on fire.

Being a firefighter on water is hard work.

Many of these heroes start as firefighters on land.

After some time, the heroes can work on a fireboat.

These heroes on the water help stop many fires.

They work to keep everyone safe.

Thanks, firefighters!

A Fireboat and Its Tools

Firefighters on the water use a special boat and tools to put out fires.

Firefighters stand on the boat's deck.

Big lights help the heroes see when it is dark.

Water is pumped from below up to the nozzles.

Nozzles shoot water onto fires.

Glossary

fireboat a boat used to fight fires on or near water

flames the glowing, moving parts of fire

nozzles parts of a fireboat that shoot out water

pumps pulls water from one place and pushes it to another

Index

dock 4, 6
fireboat 6–8, 10, 18, 22
flames 4
land 6, 18
nozzle 10, 22
sea 16
water 6, 10, 18, 20, 22

Read More

Kelly, Erin. *Fighting Fires (Be an Expert!).* New York: Children's Press, 2021.

Roberts, Antonia. *Firefighters (What Makes a Community?).* Minneapolis: Bearport Publishing Company, 2021.

Learn More Online

1. Go to **FactSurfer.com** or scan the QR code below.
2. Enter "**Water Firefighters**" into the search box.
3. Click on the cover of this book to see a list of websites.

About the Author

Spencer Brinker lives in Minnesota with his family, dog, and lizard.